MEET CHRIS PAUL

Basketball's CP3

Ethan Edwards

PowerKiDS
press

New York

Published in 2014 by The Rosen Publishing Group, Inc.
29 East 21st Street, New York, NY 10010

First Edition

Editors: Joshua Shadowens and Jennifer Way
Book Design: Greg Tucker
Book Layout: Kate Vlachos
Photo Research: Katie Stryker

Library of Congress Cataloging-in-Publication Data

Edwards, Ethan.
 Meet Chris Paul : basketball's CP3 / by Ethan Edwards — First edition.
    pages cm. — (All-star players)
 Includes index.
 ISBN 978-1-4777-2912-0 (library binding) — ISBN 978-1-4777-3001-0 (pbk.) —
 ISBN 978-1-4777-3072-0 (6-pack)
 1. Paul, Chris, 1985-–Juvenile literature. 2. Basketball players—United States—Biography—Juvenile literature.
 I. Title.
 GV884.P376E48 2014
 796.323092—dc23
 [B]
                          2013019053
Manufactured in the United States of America

CPSIA Compliance Information: Batch #W14PK2: For Further Information contact Rosen Publishing, New York, New York at 1-800-237-9932

Contents

Chris Paul uses different drills, tricks, and strategies to help him be one of the top point guards in the NBA.

Little Big Man

Chris Paul might be short for a **professional** basketball player, but he is a giant in the National Basketball Association, or NBA. Fans think he is one of the most exciting players in the game. Paul stands at only 6 feet (2 m) tall. This might seem tall, but it is short for NBA players.

He makes up for this lack of height by being one of the fastest and smartest **point guards** in the game. A point guard is the leader of a basketball team's **offense**. The fans of the Los Angeles Clippers have waited a long time for a leader like Paul.

All-Star Facts

Chris Paul says a prayer during the national anthem before each game.

Chris Paul was born in Lewisville, North Carolina, in 1985. He was close with his family, especially his older brother and his grandfather. Chris's brother, C. J., was also a great **athlete**. Their grandfather, a man named Nathaniel Jones and nicknamed Papa Chilly, was Chris's best friend during childhood. Chris enjoyed basketball, but he had more early success with football. He was a little too short for basketball. C. J. was the hoops star of the family.

That all changed during Chris's junior year in high school. He finally grew to nearly 6 feet (2 m) tall. Once C. J. graduated, Chris became the star of West Forsyth High School's basketball team. He led West Forsyth to a 26–4 record that year. The nation's top basketball coaches started paying attention to Chris. The Wake Forest Demon Deacons **recruited** him. Chris's family was overjoyed.

Paul has private workouts
with a famous trainer
named Idan Ravin to keep
his basketball skills sharp.
Ravin is nicknamed the
Hoops Whisperer.

Here Chris is playing in the thirtieth annual Jordan Capital Classic. Only the top high-school athletes compete in this game.

Their joy did not last long. Soon after Chris officially signed with Wake Forest, the family received news that a group of teenagers had killed Papa Chilly. The family, especially Chris, was crushed.

West Forsyth had a game on the day of the funeral, and Chris honored his grandfather by scoring exactly 61 points. He scored one point for each year of his grandfather's life.

Chris participated in many invitation-only games for top high-school athletes. Here he is playing in a Nike All-American Camp game.

Best Freshman

Wake Forest's coach Skip Prosser had high hopes for his new freshman point guard. Paul worked hard all summer before joining his college team, and he did not let Prosser down. He was one of the younger players in college hoops, but he quickly proved that he was also one of the best.

Paul averaged almost 15 points a game during his freshman year. Equally important, Paul also led the team in **assists**. All basketball players need to be good shooters. Point guards, however, must be good passers and smart leaders. Paul could read the other team's **defense**. He knew how to pass to the right teammate at exactly the right moment. Paul was so good that basketball expert Dick Vitale called him the nation's best freshman. Indiana Hoosiers coach Mike Davis said Paul was the best point guard his team played against. He even earned honors as the Atlantic Coast Conference's **Rookie** of the Year.

The Demon Deacons reached the Sweet 16 of the 2004 NCAA Men's Division I Basketball Tournament.

Paul broke five Wake Forest records during his freshman year, including those for steals, assists, free throws, free-throw percentage, and three-point percentage.

The pressure was on for Paul to improve during his sophomore season. He rose to the challenge and continued to lead the team. NBA coaches and experts watched him closely. They knew a young star when they saw one. Fans of the struggling New Orleans Hornets hoped Paul might be the star to turn their team around.

Here Paul is receiving the Arnold Palmer Award as the top 2005 athlete at Wake Forest.

After only two seasons playing for one of the best college teams in the nation, Paul was ready for the NBA. He declared for the 2005 NBA **Draft**. The NBA draft works like a **lottery**. The luckiest teams get to pick the best players first. The New Orleans Hornets had the fourth pick in the draft that year. Fortunately for them, none of the first three teams picked Paul.

All-Star Facts

Paul appeared on the National Public Radio quiz show *Wait Wait . . . Don't Tell Me* and answered every question correctly.

Here Paul is being fouled by Gerald Wallace of the Charlotte Bobcats. The Hornets went on to win the game.

Hurricane Katrina caused massive amounts of damage, but the Hornets fully returned to New Orleans for the 2007–2008 season.

The Hornets had won only 18 games during the previous season. New Orleans fans hoped that Paul could someday lead their team to the **play-offs**. However, those fans soon faced bigger concerns. In August 2005, Hurricane Katrina struck the Gulf Coast and destroyed much of the city of New Orleans. The Hornets could not play in their hometown and had to play all of their home games in Oklahoma City.

The tragedy provided the spark that Paul's new team needed. With their young point guard leading the team, the Hornets improved and won 38 games. Paul won Rookie of the Year honors. Sometimes it takes several seasons for top college stars to become good NBA players. Paul was on his way to becoming a star.

Paul won an ESPY Award for Best Breakthrough Athlete for his rookie season.

The Play-Offs and Olympic Gold

In the 2007–2008 season, Paul led the Hornets to the play-offs. The team had never won a **postseason** series before. That changed when the Hornets defeated the Dallas Mavericks in the first round. Paul and the Hornets fell short against the San Antonio Spurs in the next round, but they were finally one of the NBA's top teams.

Paul signed a three-year extension, worth $68 million, with the Hornets at the end of the 2007–2008 season.

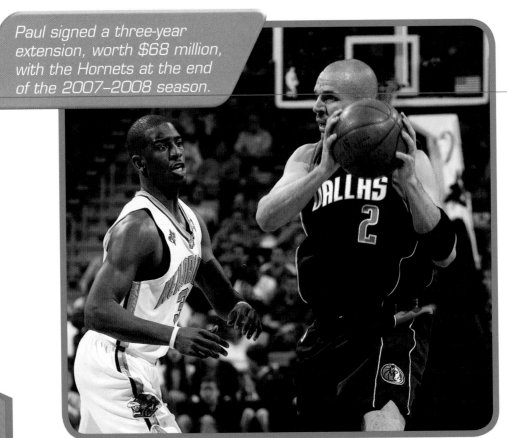

Here Paul is raising the flag after winning the gold medal at the 2008 Beijing Olympics.

Paul represented his country in 2008 by playing for the US Men's Basketball Team during the Beijing Olympic Games. Paul was not the starting point guard. He was the backup for the great Jason Kidd. Paul played well when he had the chance and helped the US team win the gold medal.

As all fans know, change is a constant part of professional sports. Paul finished the 2010–2011 season as one of the game's biggest stars. The Hornets could not afford to sign him to a new contract. It looked like Paul would be traded to the Los Angeles Lakers. This thrilled Lakers fans, but fans of other teams did not want to see Lakers superstar Kobe Bryant joined by one of the best point guards in the game. In the end, Paul did move to Los Angeles but not to play for the Lakers. He joined the city's other team, the Clippers. Just like the Hornets, the Clippers needed a new star to turn their team's luck around.

Here Paul is playing against the Dallas Mavericks for his new team, the Clippers.

The Clippers were building a team around a young **power forward** named Blake Griffin. All he needed was a great point guard. Paul immediately played well with the younger superstar, and the Clippers finished the 2011–2012 season with a record that was good enough to get them into the play-offs. They won the first-round series against the Memphis Grizzlies, but they eventually fell short against a very tough San Antonio Spurs team. Clippers fans were disappointed by the early postseason exit, but they were excited about the future of their team.

Chris Paul and Blake Griffin are considered to be the leaders of the Clippers. Other players look to them for guidance and team standards.

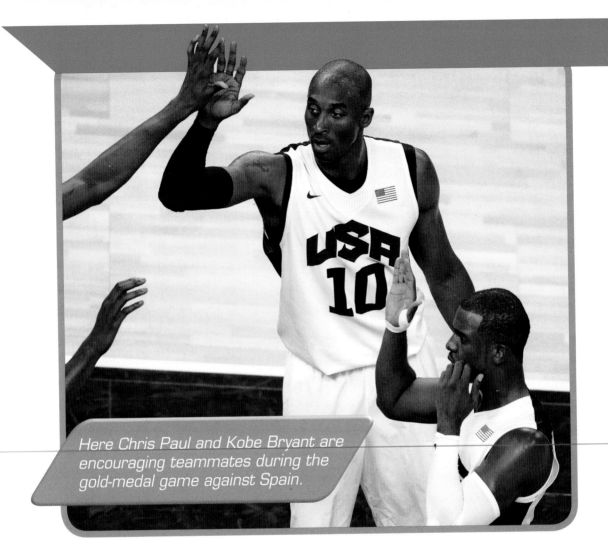

Here Chris Paul and Kobe Bryant are encouraging teammates during the gold-medal game against Spain.

Following the 2011–2012 season, Paul once again had the chance to play for the US Olympic team. He joined a roster of the best NBA players, including LeBron James and Kobe Bryant. This time the games were in London, and Paul would now serve as starting point guard.

Paul played like a star and helped America's team win the gold in a close game against Spain.

Paul had little time to celebrate his success in the London Games. It was time to get ready for the 2012–2013 season. He continued to prove himself a great leader for the Clippers. Once again, he and Griffin led the Clippers to the postseason.

Here are Paul and Griffin playing against the Indiana Pacers in a 2013 game.

Paul participates in many events as the head of the CP3 Foundation, which aids programs for Hurricane Katrina victims.

CP3

Chris has valued the bonds of family and friendship since his childhood. He married Jada Crawley in 2011. They have two children, Christopher Emmanuel Paul II and Camryn Alexis Paul. Chris and Jada met when they attended college together at Wake Forest.

Chris remains close with his brother, C. J. Chris goes by the nickname CP3 because his father's nickname is CP1, and his brother's is CP2. It just so happens that Chris wears the number three on his jersey.

All-Star Facts

You might see Paul off the court starring in **commercials** for Powerade, Nike, Right Guard, and State Farm Insurance.

Top Point Guard

Chris Paul quickly made his mark on the NBA. He is one of the smartest and fastest point guards on the court. In fact, many experts believe he is the best point guard in the NBA.

Paul's talents make it easy to forget that he is so much shorter than most of the other players in the game. It's hard to believe there was even a time when no one dreamed he could be a basketball star. Paul succeeds because of his constant hard work and excellent leadership skills. He is fortunate to share the court with great players, but he knows that great players are nothing without a great leader.

Paul agreed to a five-year extension, worth $107 million, with the Los Angeles Clippers in 2013.

Team: Los Angeles Clippers
Position: Point Guard
Uniform Number: 3
Born: May 6, 1985
Height: 6 feet (2 m)
Weight: 185 pounds (84 kg)

Season	Team	Points per Game	Rebounds per Game	Assists per Game	Free-Throw Percentage
2005–2006	Hornets	16.1	5.1	7.8	.847
2006–2007	Hornets	17.3	4.4	8.9	.818
2007–2008	Hornets	21.1	4.0	11.6	.851
2008–2009	Hornets	22.8	5.5	11.0	.868
2009–2010	Hornets	18.7	4.2	10.7	.847
2010–2011	Hornets	15.9	4.1	9.8	.878
2011–2012	Clippers	19.8	3.6	9.1	.861

Glossary

assists (uh-SISTS) Passes that let a teammate score points.

athlete (ATH-leet) Someone who takes part in sports.

commercials (kuh-MER-shulz) TV or radio messages trying to sell things.

defense (DEE-fents) When a team tries to stop the other team from scoring.

draft (DRAFT) The selection of people for a special purpose.

lottery (LAH-tuh-ree) The drawing of lots used to decide something. Lots are objects used as counters in a lottery.

offense (O-fents) When a team tries to score points in a game.

play-offs (PLAY-ofs) Games played after the regular season ends to see who will play in the championship game.

point guards (POYNT GAHRDZ) Basketball players who direct their teams' forward plays on the court.

postseason (pohst-SEE-zun) Games played after the regular season.

power forward (POW-er FOR-werd) A basketball player who mostly tries to control play near the basket.

professional (pruh-FESH-nul) Someone who is paid for what he or she does.

recruited (rih-KROOT-ed) Convinced people to join a group.

rookie (RU-kee) A new major-league player.

Index

Websites

Due to the changing nature of Internet links, PowerKids Press has developed an online list of websites related to the subject of this book. This site is updated regularly. Please use this link to access the list:
www.powerkidslinks.com/asp/paul/